Summary:

Predictably Irrational

The Hidden Forces That Shape Our Decisions

By: Dan Ariely

Proudly Brought to you by:

Text Copyright © Readtrepreneur

Legal & Disclaimer

The information contained in this book is not designed to replace or take the place of any form of medicine or professional medical advice. The information in this book has been provided for educational and entertainment purposes only.

The information contained in this book has been compiled from sources deemed reliable, and it is accurate to the best of the Author's knowledge; however, the Author cannot guarantee its accuracy and validity and cannot be held liable for any errors or omissions. Changes are periodically made to this book. You must consult your doctor or get professional medical advice before using any of the suggested remedies, techniques, or information in this book. Images used in this book are not the same as of those of the actual book. This is a totally separate and different entity from that of the original book titled: "Predictably Irrational"

Upon using the information contained in this book, you agree to hold harmless the Author from and against any damages, costs, and expenses, including any legal fees potentially resulting from the application of any of the information provided by this guide. This disclaimer applies to any damages or injury caused by the use and application, whether directly or indirectly, of any advice or information presented, whether for breach of contract, tort, negligence, personal injury, criminal intent, or under any other cause of action.

You agree to accept all risks of using the information presented inside this book. You need to consult a professional medical practitioner in order to ensure you are both able and healthy enough to participate in this program.

Table of Contents

A Note to Readers

In this section, author Dan Ariely welcomes readers to his book *Predictably Irrational: The Hidden Forces That Shape Our Decisions.*

He narrates how he has observed the inconsistencies in the actions of humans, including the way they make decisions. He has tried to study these irrational actions, with the aim of coming up with methods that would improve our decision-making skills and eventually lessen the mistakes that we repeatedly commit.

His interest in studying this aspect has led him to learn more about behavioral economics. He studied human idiosyncrasies, asking himself, why do we continue to accept false beliefs despite knowing that they are not true? Why do we prevent ourselves from telling a lie every time we are reminded of the Ten Commandments, even if nobody could possibly know that we are lying? What is the impact of emotions on the way we make decisions? With these interesting questions alone, we would know that Ariely and his team of researchers indeed enjoyed assessing their study subjects in their quest for answers.

Nonetheless, Ariely adds that he also experienced dissent in his experiments on irrationality specifically from professional investors. However, the 2008 global financial crisis opened up opportunities for people to learn more about behavioral economics. Yes, the crisis was truly a distressing time but it also opened up opportunities for people to consider better ideas to avoid making the same mistakes.

He mentions that even writing a book in this day and age, in which e-mail and blogging are highly prevalent, allows him to study more about human behavior.

Introduction

How an Injury Led Me to Irrationality and to the Research Described Here

Ariely recalls being told by a number of people that he has a unique perception of the world. This "gift" allowed him to enjoy his research career, specifically in finding what impacts the decisions we make in our daily lives.

He poses questions such as:

Why does a one-cent aspirin prevent us from curing our headache, but a 50-cent aspirin quickly takes our headache away?

Why do we always find an urgent need to purchase things we don't actually require?

Why do we tell ourselves that we will finally go on a diet but still keep on eating anyway?

Ariely promises to answer these questions by the end of his book and explain to us its connection to our business life, personal life, and, basically, our life in general.

For instance, the "effectiveness" of a 50-cent aspirin may have something to do not only with our choice of medicine but also with the issue on health insurance. Perhaps, if everyone is consistently reminded of the Ten Commandments, then the Enron-like fraud may have been prevented. All these are explained by the author through scientific studies, results, and anecdotes.

In this section, Ariely also narrates that his interest in studying this field of behavioral economics began after meeting an accident when he was only 18 years old, wherein an explosion caused him to have third-degree burns. This accident allowed him to experience various types of pain. His stay in the hospital gave him the opportunity to be with different types of people and learn more about different attitudes and behaviors. Soon, when he began his life as a college student, he found himself quickly relating all his experiences to his college lessons about the physiology of the brain. Eventually, he expanded the scope of his experiments, highly focusing on assessing cases about people committing mistakes repeatedly.

Ariely's book mainly focuses on people's irrationalities as we all go through the journey of life, and it is through the field of behavioral science that he enables himself to study all about it.

Behavioral economics, also known as judgment and decision making, focuses on both economics and psychology, and, therefore, widely differs from conventional economics. Through behavioral economics, Ariely has not only studied about people's behaviors but also about our capability to make decisions. Through his studies, he has learned that people are not merely irrational, but are "predictably irrational" in general. Our illogicality consistently transpires whether we act as citizens of our country, as lawmakers, as businessmen, or as consumers.

Ariely mentions that each chapter of the book is based on several studies he conducted with his colleagues.

Chapter 1 explains our habit of comparing things that are conveniently comparable and shaking off those that bring inconvenience. Chapter 2 talks about how the initial decisions we make eventually become part of our long-term behavior, while Chapter 3 ponders on why we tend to get excited over free products and services.

Chapter 4 offers information on social norms and market norms. In Chapter 5, Ariely examines the impact of sexual arousal on human behavior, while in Chapter 6, he discusses the tendency of people to procrastinate.

Chapter 7 focuses on how and why the value of a thing is always higher in the eyes of the owner, while Chapter 8 ponders on our tendency to grab all available options right in front of us, leaving us emotionally, mentally, financially, and physically exhausted. Chapter 9 dissects the effect of expectations on our lives, while Chapter 10 examines the correlation of expectations to both objective and subjective experiences.

Chapter 11 talks about the tendency of people to become dishonest, while Chapter 12 looks into the correlation between money and honesty. Lastly, in Chapter 13, Ariely offers his views on behavioral economics, human behavior, and predictable irrationality.

FREE BONUSES

P.S. Is it okay if we overdeliver?

Here at Readtrepreneur Publishing, we believe in overdelivering way beyond our reader's expectations. Is it okay if we overdeliver?

Here's the deal, we're going to give you an extremely condensed PDF summary of the book which you've just read and much more...

What's the catch? We need to trust you... You see, we want to overdeliver and in order for us to do that, we've to trust our reader to keep this bonus a secret to themselves? Why? Because we don't want people to be getting our exclusive PDF summaries even without buying our books itself. Unethical, right?

Ok. Are you ready?

Firstly, remember that your book is code: "**READ66**".

Next, visit this link: <u>http://bit.ly/exclusivepdfs</u>

Everything else will be self explanatory after you've visited: <u>http://bit.ly/exclusivepdfs</u>.

We hope you'll enjoy our free bonuses as much as we enjoyed preparing it for you!

CHAPTER 1: The Truth about Relativity

Why Everything Is Relative – Even When It Shouldn't Be

Ariely begins Chapter 1 by narrating his experience of stumbling upon an advertisement posted by the magazine "Economist" on its website, encouraging visitors to subscribe. The online annual subscription costs cheap, the print annual subscription costs way more, and interestingly, the online and print annual subscription package costs the same as the print subscription only. To illustrate:

Online subscription – US$59.00

Print subscription – US$125.00

Online and print subscription – US$125.00

Ariely then turned this into an interesting research participated by 100 students. Obviously, most of the participants chose the online and print subscription package.

However, their choice suddenly changed when Ariely trimmed down the options to this:

Online subscription – US$59.00

Online and print subscription – US$125.00

Apparently, the print subscription of US$125.00 was a decoy that sent majority of the participants to choose the online and print subscription package. When it was removed from the options, the participants began to opt for the cheapest subscription package.

This is indeed an example of being predictably irrational.

To simply explain relativity, it is our innate ability to look at things and compare them with other things. A more complicated explanation is that relativity is our innate ability to compare things that are conveniently comparable and fend off those that are complicated.

An example of this is when you are choosing a country to spend your vacation in. To make it easier, you have trimmed down your choices to Paris and Rome. Your travel agent then presents you with packages that have similar rates – all include free breakfast, tours, hotel accommodations, and airfare.

In most cases, choosing between Paris and Rome is not an easy decision to make as both are well known tourist spots. However, this dilemma might not be too difficult to solve if, for instance, the travel agent would include another Rome package without the free breakfast. To illustrate:

Paris package – with free breakfast

Rome package – with free breakfast

Rome package – without free breakfast

Apparently, if two of the three packages feature Rome, wherein one does not offer free breakfast, you would definitely choose the Rome package with free breakfast. Moreover, seeing two Rome packages will even make you ignore the Paris package. Obviously, the Rome package without the free breakfast is simply a decoy that helps in you decision making. The decoy, indeed, is the key in our decisions – and we may not even aware of that.

Ariely also recalls his conversation with a top executive wherein the latter talked about his young employee who complained about his salary. The young employee stated that his officemates earned higher salaries than he did but he performed way better than them.

With these examples, it seems that relativity does allow us to easily make life decisions. However, our tendency to compare one thing from another is a manifestation of envy and jealousy.

But not with Hotornot.com co-founder James Hong, who sold his Porsche Boxster and replaced it with a Toyota Prius. He emphasized that owning a Boxster would only make him want to own a 911, and it would only eventually make him want to own a Ferrari.

In other words, the more things we acquire, the more things we want to have in life. We never seem to get satisfied and the only way to address this is to break the relativity cycle.

CHAPTER 2: The Fallacy of Supply and Demand

Why the Price of Pearls – and Everything Else – Is Up in the Air

In this chapter, Ariely begins by narrating how black pearls have come to be an expensive type of jewelry.

By the end of World War II, Italian Salvador Assael was taught by his father and Swiss watch merchant James Assael how to barter wrist watches for Japanese pearls because, at that time, the Japanese people needed to acquire wrist watches but they did not have any money to buy. What they only had at that time were pearls. Salvador then learned to successfully transact with the Japanese which eventually led him to be known as the "Pearl King".

In the 1970s, Salvador met Frenchman Jean-Claude Brouillet and his Tahitian wife who both introduced him to Tahitian black pearls. Soon, Brouillet and Salvador found themselves engaged in the black pearl business. However, they did not seem to have much luck in their initial efforts to market such pearls. The pearls did not seem to be of good quality and nobody was buying from them.

This situation could have easily made Salvador give up. Instead, he waited until they could produce better black pearls which he then showed to his gemstone dealer friend Harry Winston. Winston agreed to Salvador's marketing strategy of displaying the black pearls in his store and attaching a high price tag to it. Salvador also ran a print advertisement featuring black pearls alongside emeralds, rubies, and diamonds. Today, Tahitian black pearl jewelries are worn by notable celebrities worldwide.

This buying behavior of consumers can be compared to the behavior of goslings. Did you know that baby geese, or goslings, automatically become attached to the first moving thing that they chance upon? Of course, in most cases, the first moving thing that they run into is their mother. However, in a study conducted by naturalist Konrad Lorenz, he studied the behavior of goslings by becoming the first moving thing that they saw. Evidently, he was followed by the goslings constantly until they reached adolescence. Such natural phenomenon is what we commonly know now as imprinting.

Having said that, is it safe to say that the human brain works the same way as that of a gosling? Ariely then cites a related example.

When you walk past a restaurant and see people standing in line by the door, your initial impression is that the restaurant must be serving sumptuous food. Who knows? It must also have excellent customer service! So, you fall in line too. Eventually, another person stood behind you. Another one joined... And another until there are more than 15 people standing in line behind you in less than 10 minutes. This particular type of behavior is called herding.

Ariely emphasizes that these scenarios have bigger connotations than mere consumer preference. He correlates this with the traditional economic assumption that market prices rely on the forces of supply and demand. He also explains that the relationship between supply and demand is also based on memory and does not merely end in consumer preferences.

With that, he suggests that there is probably a need to consider other areas in establishing market prices if relying on the law of supply and demand isn't enough, and also in maximizing our utility if free-market mechanisms do not offer much certainty.

CHAPTER 3: The Cost of Zero Cost

Why We Often Pay Too Much When We Pay Nothing

Chapter 3 is all about the irrational excitement felt by consumers when they are being offered free products or services.

You have probably accepted a FREE Coffee Bean Package Coupon even if you do not drink coffee. You are probably one of those customers of a buffet restaurant who stuff as much food as you can in your mouth even if you are already overwhelmingly glutted. In other words, the things that we never thought of buying or consuming suddenly become amazingly appealing to us as soon as they are offered to us for free.

In an experiment conducted by Ariely with Massachusetts Institute of Technology PhD student Kristian Shampanier and University of Toronto professor Nina Mazar, they studied consumer behavior by selling two types of chocolates – Hershey's Kisses and Lindt truffles. Lindt truffles are manufactured by a Swiss firm that is known for using various types of fine cocoas in their products, while Hershey's Kisses are known to be delectable but more ordinary compared to Lindt.

They initially offered a Kiss for one cent and a Lindt truffle for 15 cents. The result? Over 70 percent of the consumers bought Lindt truffles while the rest bought Hershey's Kisses. Apparently, majority of the consumers looked at the price and used it as basis for the quality of the product – the more expensive the chocolate, the more of high-quality it is. Indeed, it was a rational move.

In the second phase of their experiment, Ariely and his colleagues lowered the price of the chocolates by one cent – the Lindt truffle became 14 cents while the Kiss became FREE. The result? Majority of the consumers opted to get free Kisses and totally ignored the Lindt truffles. Now, where did all the rationality go?

This is no different when you visit a sports store to purchase a pair of socks – the type with high quality padded heel ideal for basketball. A few minutes later, you walked out of the store, not with the pair of socks you initially wanted to buy, but with two cheaper pairs of socks that were offered at 50% discount each. In this case, you gave up quality as you were enticed by the discount. Is this what you call a better deal?

How come when products are offered for free, people tend to become irrational?

All of us will probably agree that there are always advantages and advantages in everything we do. However, when we are offered something free, we tend to forget about the disadvantages. We feel as if we are always on the upside when we get something at no cost.

Ariely also explains that the concept of zero indeed has an impact on time. For example, we may be enticed to stand in line for 45 minutes just to get free ice cream when we could have earned a living if we used 45 minutes of our time to close a business deal instead.

Indeed, "free" is such a powerful thing. Perhaps, the government may want to consider free electric car registration and inspection fees if they want people to shift to electric vehicles. Perhaps, free medical procedures should be imposed to prevent, if not eliminate, the occurrence of serious illnesses.

CHAPTER 4: The Cost of Social Norms

Why We Are Happy to Do Things, but Not When We Are Paid to Do Them

In Chapter 4, Ariely examines human behavior through social and market norms. In most cases, social norms prevail when interacting with friends and family members, while market norms prevail during business dealings. You cannot pay your mother-in-law for preparing dinner for you, but you can definitely give her a gift to express your appreciation. You cannot pay a golf instructor friend for voluntarily giving golf tips, but you can pay him if you officially hire him as your golf coach. In other words, social norms do not have any monetary equivalent whereas market norms are associated with costs and benefits, interests, rents, prices, and wages.

Ariely uses sex in one of his examples, indicating that it could be an example of both social and market norms. Sex is free among spouses and no husband has probably paid his wife for having sex with him. But in another context, there is what we call market sex wherein people pay for it. Obviously, this is commonly known as prostitution.

In an experiment Ariely conducted with University of St. Thomas professor James Heyman, they explored the impact of market and social norms on people by dividing their participants into several groups and instructing them to do a similar task.

The task was simple. In the computer screen, there was a circle on the left side and a square on the right side. Participants were asked to drag the circle into the square. Every time the circle would be successfully placed inside the square, a new circle would pop up on the left side of the screen which would again be dragged by the participant into the square. This should be done repeatedly. The goal was to drag as many circles as they could inside the square.

Ariely and Heyman offered five dollars to each participant of the first group, while 50 cents was offered to each participant of the second group. The third group, however, was offered nothing. Instead, they were merely instructed to participate in the study.

Can you guess which group performed well?

If you guessed the third group, well, you are correct.

The participants who received five dollars each dragged over 155 circles on the average, while those who received 50 cents each dragged 100 circles only on the average. The participants who were not paid at all, however, performed way better than the paid participants, dragging roughly 179 circles into the square. This only goes to show that people tend to perform better when they are merely asked to help or a favor is being asked from them. When people are paid for what they do, they tend to limit their actions which heavily depend on the amount given to them. Apparently, money influences their behavior.

This human behavior then poses questions related to the existence of social norms in the workplace. Do social norms actually exist in offices? Are such social values as trust and loyalty still prevalent among employees? Or is the productivity of the United States dependent on the salaries received by workers?

CHAPTER 5: The Influence of Arousal

Why Hot Is Much Hotter Than We Realize

In Chapter 5, Ariely offers information on research focusing on the effect of sexual arousal on human behavior. By understanding this topic, Ariely hopes to help society address such issues as HIV-AIDS and teenage pregnancy, among others.

In one of the experiments, Ariely and his team looked for participants at the University of California, Berkeley, wherein their ad specifically targeted male study subjects who were at least 18 years of age and heterosexual. The ad clearly indicated that the men would be participating in a study about arousal and decision making, that the research procedures would involve pornographic material, and that they would get paid US$10 for every session.

Ariely and his team began the experiment as soon as they had completed their 25 participants. Each participant was given an Apple iBook computer with a keyboard which they would set up in their bedroom where they would answer a series of questions. Among the questions that they needed to answer were, would they agree to have sex with someone they hated? Would they want to tie someone up or to get tied up during sex? Would they get frustrated if they partner merely wanted to be kissed? Would they tell a woman "I love you" just so she would agree to have sex?

In the first session, the participants would simply answer these questions while they were in bed. In the second session, they were asked to answer the same set of questions while they were sexually aroused. They were even asked to browse through pornographic materials before answering them.

One of the participants was a college student named Roy. He was a straight A-student, athletic, kind, and, at that time, was planning to take up medicine. Apparently, he was someone a mother-in-law would ever dream of. At first, the impression was, his behavior in this experiment would be different from the rest who were all average college students. But Roy's answers were no different from theirs.

In one of the questions answered by the participants, it showed that their willingness to do various sexual activities was higher when they were aroused than when they were not. In another question which they answered when they were not aroused, they said that they would definitely not engage themselves in immoral activities. But they confessed otherwise when they answered it while they were aroused.

This goes to show that if men are not aroused, they indeed express their respect for women, their fear of getting HIV or AIDS, their awareness that they should wear a condom, and so on. But if they are aroused, morality and conservatism disappear altogether. The conclusion here is we, therefore, tend to make wrong decisions when we are gripped by extreme emotion – and even a man that any mother-in-law would ever dream of is definitely not an exception.

Ariely emphasizes that it is important for each one of us to understand the changes in our emotional state as this has a connection with the decisions we make in our daily lives.

CHAPTER 6: The Problem of Procrastination and Self-Control

Why We Can't Make Ourselves Do What We Want to Do

In Chapter 6, Ariely focuses on the issue of procrastination.

Chapter 5 discussed how emotions grip us and tend to change our perspectives. Apparently, emotion is also the root of procrastination. For instance, you want to save money and you tell yourself that you will start saving today. But you pass by a shopping mall and, there, you see your dream clothes being offered at a discount. You then tell yourself that you will just start saving tomorrow.

It is no different when you tell yourself that you will engage in a weight loss program starting today. But your favorite TV series is on Netflix and a chocolate cake is sitting in your fridge waiting to be devoured. So, you decide to just exercise and diet tomorrow.

In a study conducted by Ariely and INSEAD professor Klaus Wertenbroch at Massachusetts Institute of Technology, Ariely required his students to submit three papers during the semester. In his first class, he asked his students to set their own deadline. In his second class, he asked his students to submit their papers on or before the last day of the semester. In his third class, he gave his students strict deadlines for each of the three papers to be submitted. The objective was to determine which class would achieve the best final grade.

When the semester ended and the papers were checked, it was found out that the class with strict deadlines got the best grades. The class who chose their own deadlines placed second, and the class who were asked to submit their papers at the end of the semester got the worst grades of all.

So, what do these findings indicate? It tells us that procrastination indeed exists among students, that giving restrictions to their freedom alleviates procrastination, and providing them with tools equips them to perform better.

These findings indeed have a connection to our daily lives. This study emphasizes that mastering self-control

19

and resistance to temptation are human objectives that we can't seem to achieve. We have always been aware of this weakness but we never seem to address it, and so we find ourselves in the same predicament over and over again.

There are quite a number of situations wherein we may catch ourselves procrastinating. Let's identify two of them.

Healthcare

We all know that preventive medicine is best for all of us as it is the most cost-effective approach of all. Preventive medicine means undergoing medical exams regularly to detect health issues and treat them as early as possible before they get worse. But the problem is we don't undergo medical exams at all unless it is required, usually by company policies, or unless we feel that something is already wrong. This tendency to procrastinate is something serious as it already involves our health.

Savings

As mentioned earlier, we always tell ourselves how we want to save money but we opt to delay our plan every time we see something at the mall being offered at a discount. In fact, sometimes, even if it is not offered at a discount, we buy it as long as we feel the urge to do so. Indeed, we tend to forget our plan to save up.

CHAPTER 7: The High Price of Ownership

Why We Overvalue What We Have

In Chapter 7, Ariely ponders on how people value the things they own.

Have you ever wondered why a person who sells his house values his property more than the buyer? The same can be said for a person who sells his automobile – he envisions a price that is higher than what the buyer is willing to pay. Ariely and INSEAD professor Ziv Carmon conducted an experiment related to this.

At Duke University, in order to watch a game at its basketball stadium, students had to fall in line to register and join the lottery. This lottery was their only chance to win tickets to watch the game. As part of the experiment, Ariely and Carmon talked to several students who won and who did not win the lottery. The objective was to determine how much these students valued the tickets.

William was a student who did not win a ticket to watch the game. Ariely called him up and asked how much he would be willing to pay if he would be sold a ticket. William answered "US$175."

Joseph was a student who won a ticket, and when Ariely called him up to ask the price for which he would be willing to sell his ticket, his reply was "US$3,000."

Joseph and William were only two of over a hundred students that Ariely and Carmon contacted. The findings of this experiment indicated that those who did not win in the lottery were definitely willing to buy tickets but were not willing to spend over US$200 for each ticket. On the other hand, those who won tickets were willing to sell each ticket for not lower than US2,000.

Apparently, ticket owners and non-ticket owners valued the ticket differently. But, logically speaking, everyone should value it in the same way as they were talking about one basketball game here. This only goes to show that ownership strongly affects our lives.

In relation to this experiment, let's talk about several irrational idiosyncrasies in the nature of human beings.

First, people fall in love and get emotionally attached with what they own. In fact, when we sell our car, we recall every trip we made and all other memories that go with it.

Second, when people price their possession, their computation includes what they may lose instead of what will be gained. Using the basketball game ticket as an example, the students who won tickets focused on the fact that they would not be able to watch the game if they sold the ticket – they did not focus on the fact that they would earn money to purchase something else.

Third, people tend to expect that their possession will be valued by others in the same way – that others will also take into consideration their memories, emotions, and feelings. Unfortunately, that is not the case. Others do not view the world as we perceive it.

Ownership has its own oddities. Ariely further explains this by talking about virtual ownership and citing online auction as an example.

For instance, you join an online auction to bid for a wristwatch, and on the first day, you are the highest bidder. On the second and third day, you're still the highest bidder. The fourth time you logged on, you're still the number one bidder. At this point, you start imaging the watch on your wrist and showing it off to your friends and family. However, after logging on for the fifth time, someone else tops your bid! But because you are already taking ownership of the item, you increase your bid and make sure no one else can top it. In this scenario, you spend more than your budget all because of your sense of ownership.

Ownership doesn't only apply to material things – it can also be about our perspectives. We take ownership of what we believe in and even value it higher than its worth.

Economist and philosopher Adam Smith once talked about how ownership forms part of our lives. Therefore, we might not be able to address whatever oddity that ownership has. However, being aware of the ills of ownership might help in improving the way we live.

CHAPTER 8: Keeping Doors Open

Why Options Distract Us from Our Main Objective

Chapter 8 focuses on the habit of people to keep as many options as possible.

We may not be aware of it, but we have this tendency to always think of options when we buy something. For instance, you need to buy a computer because you need to use Microsoft Word often. So, you go to a computer store and choose to buy an expensive computer with all these state-of-the-art features, thinking that you might need those high-tech features in the future.

Another example is when you decide to buy a high-definition TV that is offered with a life insurance policy – not because you need a TV but because you need life insurance. Besides, your TV at home is old and buying as early as now will free you from future problems.

Another example is enrolling your child in several activities such as tae kwon do, French language classes, piano lessons, and basketball because he might need all these in the future.

It is good that we anticipate things but, unconsciously, we don't realize that this habit makes us give up some things. Buying a computer system that has more features than what we really need makes us spend more than our budget. Do you think buying a TV that is offered with insurance is indeed a wise decision? What about your decision to enroll your child in a lot of extra-curricular activities? Does this still leave you time to play and bond with your child?

Another example of this is the love problem experienced by Ariely's student named Dana. She met a man whom she liked better than her long-time boyfriend. She could not let go of her long-time boyfriend for fear that she might eventually realize that she loved him more than the new one.

So, why do we have this habit of keeping so many doors open? Why do we like complicating things by finding as many available options as possible?

In the quest for answers, Ariely and Yale University professor Jiwoong Shin conducted studies related to keeping options open. They created a computer program that featured three doors which the participant could enter with just a click. Once inside the room, the participant would earn money for each click he makes. For instance, if one of the rooms offered US$1 for every click, then the participant would earn US$10 for 10 clicks.

This was tried by a student named Albert who began clicking as many as he could as soon as he entered one of the rooms. Then, he tried the other door too which allowed him to earn more. He decided to enter the last room in hopes that he would earn even more. Unfortunately, the last room offered a lesser amount so he quickly went back to the second door to generate more money.

In the next experiment, Ariely and Shin decided to change the game. If in the first experiment, the participant could enter any room at any time, in the second experiment, the room would disappear if it would not be visited after making 12 clicks. In other words, the participant would need to click all three doors before he reached 12 clicks should he want to visit all rooms.

This was tried by a student named Sam who hurriedly clicked from one door to another. This resulted to earning lesser money than what she could have possibly generated if only she decided to stick with one room.

If we apply this to our daily lives, do you think that jumping from one option to another is an efficient approach? Apparently, doing so is stressful. Moreover, it doesn't seem to be economical. We might want to change this habit and make our lives less complicated.

CHAPTER 9: The Effect of Expectations

Why the Mind Gets What It Expects

Suppose you are watching a game of your favorite football team, Philadelphia Eagles, against New York Giants, the favorite team of your friend. You witness the referee signal a touchdown in favor of the Eagles. However, there are protests as the receiver did not seem to place both of his feet in. You hear yourself shout that the feet were indeed in, but your friend emphasizes otherwise.

Remember, only one incident transpired but the two people who witnessed what happened viewed it in totally different ways.

Ariely, London Business School professor Marco Bertini, and Harvard Business School professor Elie Ofek created a coffee shop in one of the experiments they conducted. Free cups of coffee were offered to students in exchange for a survey that they need to complete. They were also offered coffee additives like brown sugar, white sugar, coffee creamer, and milk, and other condiments like cardamom, sweet paprika, nutmeg, and cloves, among others.

Sometimes, students were offered coffee in beautiful and fancy cups. Other times, they were offered coffee in Styrofoam cups. At the end of this experiment, it was found out that students found coffee in fancy cups more delicious than those in Styrofoam cups. In fact, they did not add any condiments anymore as they were truly satisfied with the taste.

On the other hand, students who were given coffee in Styrofoam cups kept on adding condiments in it to make it tasteful and delicious. The odd thing here was only one kind of coffee was used during the entire experiment. Apparently, how the coffee was presented indeed had a psychological effect on the students.

The same thing occurs when looking for a caterer for a wedding reception. Restaurant A takes pride in their "delectable chicken cooked Asian-style" while Restaurant B boasts of its "luscious organic chicken breast drizzled with classic merlot demi glace sauce." For sure, we will get enticed by Restaurant B's offering simply by reading the menu alone.

This also happens when we watch a movie. More often than not, we are encouraged to watch a movie because we hear great reviews about it. Then, we invite our friends, who all agree to watch with us after telling them that such movie has great reviews.

In all the experiments conducted by Ariely, he has come to learn that the people's investment in their beliefs is far stronger than anything else. If all of us will read the same history book right now, chances are that not all of us will have the same interpretation of it. Even if facts are already presented, we still try to argue with it and even stubbornly force others to believe the beliefs that we hold on to.

Apparently, this means that our investment in our perspectives somehow causes us to be blind to reality. Perhaps, if you see yourself arguing with another person, you should be open to the idea of getting the opinion of a third party. It may be a little difficult to accept the perspective of a third party, especially if it opposes your own perspective, but it can bring in significant benefits. Perhaps, this is something that we should try to practice.

CHAPTER 10: The Power of Price

Why a 50-Cent Aspirin Can Do What a Penny Aspirin Can't

In the previous chapter, it was discussed how expectations alter our perceptions and the way we express our appreciation for our experiences. In this chapter, Ariely further discusses how expectations can impact us by changing both our objective and subjective experiences.

Ariely begins this chapter by narrating a study conducted by cardiologist Leonard Cobb in the 1950s wherein he administered internal mammary artery ligation in a group of patients and faked such procedure in another group of patients. Surprisingly, patients from both groups told him that they all experienced immediate relief and that they did not experience any chest pain anymore. It could be mere coincidence, but all patients also complained that their chest pains returned three months after undergoing such medical procedure.

Orthopedic surgeon J.B. Moseley also conducted a study in the 1990s wherein he divided his patients (those with knee problems) into three groups. The first group underwent the standard arthroscopic surgery which included cartilage removal. The second group underwent the same surgical procedure but, this time, without cartilage removal. The third group of patients underwent a simulated surgical procedure – no medical instruments were inserted in their knee at all.

Surprisingly, and strangely, all patients – including those who did not undergo the surgery – reported pain relief and big improvements in their ability to walk.

In this regard, it can perhaps be concluded that this phenomenon has something to do with the price paid by the patients. Knowing that surgical procedures are costly, there is a psychological effect that we always expect to get healed immediately after undergoing surgery. This phenomenon is known as the placebo effect.

In the 1700s, Italian physician Gerbi strangely discovered that the secretions of a specific type of worm could cure toothaches. Hundreds of patients went to him to be treated and majority of them reported immediate relief. Up till now, there are no studies supporting that such secretions can indeed cure toothaches.

In ancient times, most medicines were placebos, indicating that mercury, dried fox lungs, bat wing, and toad's eye, among others, could cure different types of diseases. In fact, even today, all of us still believe in the magic of placebos one way or the other. Our headache suddenly disappears after taking a pill. We suddenly feel better after talking to a doctor, but we feel far better after talking to a highly acclaimed specialist.

At times, we feel that the efficacy of placebos is odd, but, nonetheless, they are effective because of our strong belief that they are.

To digress a bit from the field of medicine, we seem to have a similar experience when we talk about furniture. Is a US$4,000 couch truly more comfortable that a US$400 couch? If we tried sitting on both without looking at the price tag, would we find any difference?

Is a pair of designer trousers far more comfortable than a pair bought from Wal-Mart?

In the marketing profession, placebos do have an impact too because marketers need to hype their products.

Marketers have to assess their skills when they are promoting their products – do they stretch out the truth? Or do they carry out subtle lies?

CHAPTER 11: The Context of Our Character, Part I

Why We Are Dishonest, and What We Can Do about It

In this Chapter, Ariely begins by identifying two types of dishonesty. First is the type committed by burglars, robbers, automobile theft, and others who are considered criminals in the public eye. Second is the type committed by people who are considered honest in general. They are those who fake property losses for insurance claims, they are politicians who accept extravagant trips from lobbyists, and they are executives who augments his final pay by backdating stock options, among many others. Who do you think gets more money? Those who are publicly known as career criminals? Or those who are considered to be honest people?

To check the honesty of people, Ariely conducted a study at the Harvard Business School wherein several MBA students were divided into four groups. All students were made to answer 50 trivial questions such as "Who is the goddess of love in Greek mythology?",

"Who is the author of Moby-Dick?", and "In the whole world, what is considered to be the longest river?" among others. It was a multiple-choice type of test wherein each student would be given 10 cents for every correct answer. However, the setup varied for each group.

For the first group, the students were initially asked to write their answers in their worksheet and were subsequently instructed to transfer their answers to a bubble sheet. Both their worksheet and their bubble sheet were submitted to their proctor.

For the second group, the instructions were basically the same except that the bubble sheet was already pre-marked – the correct answers were shaded in grey color. Meaning, if the correct answer in item no. 1 was B and the student's answer was C, then there should be two markings in that item. For every correct answer in the bubble sheet, a student was paid 10 cents. While the bubble sheet was the basis for getting paid, the students were nonetheless requested to submit both their worksheet and their bubble sheet.

For the third group, the setup was basically the same as that of the second group. The main difference was, the students were instructed to shred the worksheet on which they initially wrote their answers. They were only required to submit the bubble sheet to their proctor.

For the fourth group, the setup was basically the same as that of the third group. But, this time, students were instructed to shred both their worksheet and their bubble sheet after counting all their correct answers. They were then instructed to personally withdraw their earnings in a jar full of coins placed inside the classroom.

The first group which did not have any opportunity to cheat averagely scored 33 out of the 50 questions. The second group, whose bubble sheet was pre-marked but students had to submit both their worksheet and bubble sheet to the proctor, averagely scored higher than the first group. Perhaps, these Harvard students were smarter than those in the first group?

The average scores of the students under the third and fourth groups were remarkably higher too than the first group but almost similar to the average score of the second group.

This basically means that even honest people have the tendency to cheat if and when opportunity presents itself to them.

How would being honest benefit us as American citizens? Well, it can prevent doctors from instructing us to undergo medical tests just so they would earn money, and it could prevent the U.S. Congress from specifying their own salaries, among many other things.

CHAPTER 12: The Context of Our Character, Part II

Why Dealing with Cash Makes Us More Honest

Chapter 12 begins with an experiment conducted by Ariely to test the honesty of the students staying at MIT dormitories.

One morning, he placed a six-pack Coke in a communal refrigerator, and in a span of three days, all six cans of Coke were gone. In another communal refrigerator, he placed a plate of money amounting to US$6. Surprisingly, the plate remained untouched after three days. So, what does this mean?

This apparently means that people would rather cheat without any direct contact with money. Here are several examples: a company tweaks their accounting practices to cover up fraud; stock options are backdated so that executives could get higher salaries; and physicians and their spouses are sent on lavish vacations by a pharmaceutical company. To further study this phenomenon, Ariely conducted an experiment at an MIT cafeteria.

The students were all asked to answer 20 math problems and would earn 50 cents for every correct answer. Basically, this experiment had a similarity to the one discussed in the previous chapter. The students in Group 1 answered the questions, submitted their worksheets to their proctor, and got paid after tallying their correct answers. The students in Group 2 were instructed to shred off their worksheets and inform their proctor how many correct answers they got. Of course, they got paid for it.

The students in Group 3 were instructed the same thing – shred their worksheets and inform their proctor of their score. However, this time, the proctor gave them tokens instead of cash. These tokens would eventually be presented to another person who would then exchange the tokens for their monetary equivalent.

Out of the 20 math problems, an average of 3.5 questions was answered correctly by Group 1 and an average of 6 questions was answered correctly by Group 2.

Astonishingly, the students under Group 3 averaged 9 correct answers.

In the previous chapter, it was mentioned that honest people have the tendency to cheat if and when opportunity presents itself. In this last experiment, it was learned that honest people have the tendency to cheat even more if money is not involved directly, in spite of the fact that, when carefully thought, these non-monetary currencies such as tokens also have monetary equivalents.

In another experiment, Ariely wanted to know the views of his students when it comes to cheating. He asked them if people would tend to engage in fraud more if they deal with tokens than they would if they deal with cash. The students replied that the level of cheating would have no difference because, according to them, even the tokens represent real money.

Apparently, we are not aware that we tend to cheat more when dealing with non-monetary currencies – no, we are not conscious at all. If we were, we would realize that taking home pens and bond papers from work is cheating – so does taking someone else's can of Coke from a communal refrigerator or even backdating stock options.

CHAPTER 13: Beer and Free Lunches

What Is Behavioral Economics, and Where Are The Free Lunches?

In this final chapter, Ariely offers information on experiments he conducted on predictable irrationality. He then moves on to further discuss human behavior and behavioral economics.

Ariely and Columbia University professor Jonathan Levav conducted their experiment at the Carolina Brewery, wherein they offered free samples of beer to the customers. There were four different types of beer available, namely Summer Wheat Ale, India Pale Ale, Franklin Street Lager, and Copperline Amber Ale.

The first table they approached consisted of two men and two ladies. When asked which beer they would choose, one chose Copperline Amber Ale, one chose India Pale Ale, the other chose Franklin Street Lager, and the last one chose Summer Wheat Ale. In other words, their orders were different from one another.

In another group of customers, Ariely and Levav asked them not to say their orders aloud. Instead, they were asked to write on a piece of paper their preferred beer. Can you guess what our researchers found?

It was learned that when customers say out loud their orders, they unconsciously make sure that their orders are different from one another. Unlike when they write them down, their orders will most likely be the same. But, if you thoroughly think about the experiment, those who wrote down their orders are far more satisfied than those who said their orders aloud. Why? It is simply because of the fact that they ordered what they really liked and did not consider the orders of others.

Apparently, there is this human characteristic that may be termed as "need for uniqueness" wherein we give up the pleasure of getting what we truly want just so we can express our own uniqueness.

When talking about standard economics, it tells us that we are expected to be rational and sensible when making decisions. It tells us that when we commit mistakes, we immediately learn from them.

46

However, based on the findings gathered from all the experiments mentioned, it seems that we are not at all rational when it comes to decision-making. We cannot even say that our irrationalities are senseless or random because, in fact, they are predictable and, surprisingly, systematic. Moreover, our tendency not to be aware of the mistakes we commit makes us repeat these mistakes over and over again.

Here, Ariely points out the need to amend standard economics. He emphasizes that economics would be more sensible if it would be based NOT on the ideal behavior of people, but on the real behavior of people. In other words, economics would make more sense if we based it on how people behave in reality and not on how we expect people to behave. This indeed is behavioral economics.

Ariely thoroughly explains how the concept of free lunches differs between behavioral economics and standard economics. In standard economics, the assertion is that there are indeed no free lunches. Everyone is assumed to be logical, wherein every move is motivated by an equal amount of goods and services.

On the contrary, behavioral economics points out our susceptibility to various forces around us including shortsightedness, impertinent emotions, and other types of illogicalities.

Reflections and Anecdotes about
Some of the Chapters

Here, Ariely presents additional commentary on the topics tackled in his book. He gave several fascinating details on his experiences while writing, doing research, and going on book tours. Likewise, he provided insights on how some of the lessons have been applied in the most intriguing of ways.

One example of such is his interaction with an undergraduate who asked for dating advice. He suggested going bar-hopping with someone who's sufficiently similar in the aesthetics department yet still relatively lacking. This plays on the relative nature of evaluations, in which people tend to focus on the choices in front of them. The undergraduate was definitely pleased with the results – regardless of the ethical dilemma that came with her actions.

Ariely also gave an interesting account involving placebo. He happened to sit beside a woman who brought with her an immune-boosting supplement that's dissolved in water to create a fizzy beverage. On its label, it was touted as a "miracle cold buster" and Ariely was so pleased with it and its claims that he didn't care if it was placebo. He believed in its effects.

Eventually though, the supplement's manufacturer changed their product's label to better reflect the truth. It no longer had all the amazing claims it once had and there was a note regarding the lack of scientific proof for those that remain. While Ariely knew all along that it was placebo, the addition of such information in print is what "killed" the placebo's "potency".

Thoughts about the Subprime Mortgage Crisis and Its Consequences

In this section, Ariely presents his views on the impact of irrational behavior on the subprime mortgage crisis that transpired in the United States in 2008. He believes that irrational behavior and psychology indeed have an effect on the country's economic condition.

He talks about the ambiguous mortgage practices that were heightened by collateralized debt obligations (CDOs). The CDO issue worsened the housing market bubble deflation, which brought about declining valuations. This subsequently led the public to doubt the capabilities of the players in the financial services industry.

In 2008, Bear Stearns was acquired by JP Morgan Chase for as low as US$2 per share. This low amount resulted from a CDO-related fraud involving Bear Stearns. In the same year following such acquisition, major financial institutions that heavily bet on mortgage-backed securities, including CDOs, reported losses amounting to approximately US$500 billion. Subsequently, a number of banks were reported to be under investigation for CDO-related practices.

In the same year following both crises, Freddie Mac and Fannie Mae were officially federalized by the U.S. government to prevent bankruptcy. The government had to execute this move lest it would have a negative impact on financial markets.

Soon thereafter, the U.S. Federal Reserve allowed AIG to borrow money to avoid its collapse, Lehman Brothers announced its decision to file for Chapter 11 bankruptcy, and Bank of America acquired Merrill Lynch. Moreover, JP Morgan Chase acquired several banking subsidiaries of Washington Mutual, and the lone subsidiary that JP Morgan did not acquire filed for bankruptcy. During this time, the bailout package that U.S. President George Bush proposed was rejected by the U.S. Congress which resulted in a decline in the stock market of over 700 points. All these transpired in a span of one month.

In the following month, Wachovia was reported to be negotiating with Wells Fargo and Citigroup, while the stock market further declined by 22% as a continued effect of the bailout issue. Institutional banks were reporting their losses one after another.

If all these transpired despite applying rational economic approaches, then what else is left for us to do? What other models are we supposed to apply? As mentioned earlier, perhaps we should focus on the actual behavior of people and, from there, address whatever issues we see, instead of focusing on the supposed behavior of people and simply make them follow because, ideally, it is the rational thing to do.

In the book *The Theory of Moral Sentiments*, author Adam Smith emphasizes that economists should not neglect such aspects of human behavior as morality, feelings, and emotions. He states that these subjects should be thoroughly studied.

In connection to this, behavioral economists have been exerting their efforts to conduct more studies in hopes that they could modify standard economics, move it away from naïve psychology, and shove it to a more appropriate study of human behavior.

When talking about the mortgage crisis, we find news-casters, economists, politicians, and the public in general blaming different factors of its occurrence. Some believe that the crisis was caused by the irresponsibility of bor-rowers, while others believed that borrowers merely act-ed in accordance with what was agreed with predatory lenders.

When talking about the fall of the financial services in-dustry, we can't help but wonder about what transpired for banks and financial institutions to lose sight of the economic condition.

When it comes to the condition of the government, was trust overlooked by government officials as a pertinent economic asset?

In this section, Ariely helps you ponder on these issues.

Thanks

In this section, Ariely acknowledges the notable people who made it possible for the book *Predictably Irrational: The Hidden Forces That Shape Our Decisions* to be published.

First and foremost, he thanks all individuals involved in all the experiments he conducted. He emphasizes that these individuals are not merely researchers, research assistants, and research participants, but are actually his friends.

He thanks his colleagues in the fields of economics and psychology for their influences in his work.

He thanks Massachusetts Institute of Technology (MIT) as the majority of the book was written while he was there. Moreover, most of his research assistants and research participants were students of MIT.

He thanks his HarperCollins editor Claire Wachtel for helping him finalize his book. He also specifically thanks several individuals who made this journey as meaningful, exciting, and productive as possible.

He gives special mention to the Institute for Advanced Study at Princeton University as it was where he mostly spent time writing his book.

Lastly, he expresses his gratitude to his wife for all her patience as she repeatedly listened to his research stories every single day.

List of Collaborators

This section features the notable people who became involved in Ariely's experiments and other activities to make the publication of his book possible.

On Amir

Ariely appreciates the professor-student relationship that he has developed with Amir. Ariely is amazed of the skills and talents of Amir, and considers him as an ideal student.

Marco Bertini

Marco Bertini is a London Business School professor. He was a Harvard Business School student when he met Ariely.

Ziv Carmon

Ziv Carmon is an INSEAD professor in Singapore. Ariely thanks him for teaching him how to conduct studies and for making him realize more things about decision making. Ariely states that Carmon was his reason for enrolling at Duke University.

Shane Frederick

Shane Frederick is an MIT professor who is always engaged in lengthy discussions with Ariely about fish and sushi. He was studying in Carnegie Mellon when he met Ariely, who was then a Duke University student.

James Heyman

James Heyman is a University of St. Thomas professor in Minnesota. Ariely has learned many things from him, specifically the impact of behavioral economics on policy decisions. Heyman and Ariely were together at Berkeley University.

Leonard Lee

Leonard Lee is a Columbia University professor. When Ariely met him at MIT, he was a PhD student who focused on the topic of e-commerce. Their friendship developed only because they usually stayed up late to work on projects until they started to spend their breaks together.

Jonathan Levav

Jonathan Levav is a Columbia University professor and one of the most sociable people that Ariely has ever met.

George Loewenstein

George Loewenstein is a Carnegie Mellon University professor and one of Ariely's favorite collaborators. Ariely admires him for his creativity when conducting experiments in behavioral economics.

Nina Mazar

Nina Mazar is a University of Toronto professor as well as a fashion designer in Italy. Mazar was supposed to stay at MIT for only a few days, but she lasted for half a decade as she found it an enjoyable and interesting place for both work and study.

Elie Ofek

Elie Ofek is a Harvard Business School professor. He studied electrical engineering but ended up with a career in marketing.

Yesim Orhun

Yesim Orhun is a University of Chicago professor, whose studies on behavioral economics Ariely finds interesting and helpful.

Drazen Prelec

Drazen Prelec is an MIT professor, whom Ariely admits to being a fan of. Ariely says that Prelec is one of the most intelligent people that he has ever encountered in his lifetime.

Kristina Shampanier

Kristina Shampanier is a consultant in Boston, Massachusetts. She initially became part of MIT to be groomed as an economist. Moreover, Ariely had the privilege to work with her.

Jiwoong Shin

Jiwoong Shin is a Yale University professor described by Ariely as a "yin and yang" researcher. He has presented studies on standard economics and has also published studies on behavioral economics.

Baba Shiv

Baba Shiv is a Stanford University professor. Ariely met him when they were both in the PhD program of Duke University. Shiv has conducted studies on the impact of emotions on decision making.

Rebecca Waber

Rebecca Waber is an MIT graduate student and one of the happiest and most energetic individuals that Ariely has ever encountered in his entire life. Waber's works mainly focus on decision making and its connection with the medical field.

Klaus Wertenbroch

Klaus Wertenbroch is an INSEAD professor. Ariely and Wertenbroch were both PhD students when they met at Duke University.

About the Author

Dan Ariely founded the Center for Advanced Hindsight in the United States. Currently, he is a behavioral economics professor at Duke University and a visiting professor at the Media Laboratory of MIT. He was an Institute for Advance Study fellow at Princeton University when he wrote his book. His research has been featured in scholarly publications of various fields such as business, medicine, neuroscience, economics, and psychology. He has appeared in both television and radio news programs.

To learn more about Ariely and his work, please visit www.predictablyirrational.com.

Conclusion

The book *Predictably Irrational: The Hidden Forces That Shape Our Decisions* is our guide to realizing that we tend to be unconsciously irrational in situations in which we are expected to be rational.

The people who are expected to read the book are:

- Those who always tend to make illogical decisions

- People who doubt their decision-making skills

- Economists

- Bankers

- Executives

- Politicians

- Anyone curious about the human nature of making illogical decisions in the middle of complex scenarios

The key message of the book is to keep an open mind and be aware that there are times when we think we are making rational decisions when, in fact, we are acting otherwise. Acknowledging this fact tends to make us think twice, thrice, or even several times before making our final decision. In other words, we carefully think about our plans before we put them into action to prevent ourselves from committing mistakes. More importantly, it will prevent us from committing the same mistakes over and over again.

Actionable Advice:

The next time you find yourself caught up in making complex decisions, think about Ariely's work. Think about what you have learned and immediately apply it.

You can start by practicing decision making when you're in the mall to buy clothes. Go to the mall with a specific clothing style in mind and the exact budget for that. Stick to that design and budget even if you see other clothes being sold at a discount. Remember that you are practicing rationality here, and there is no better way to

practice this than to start in simple things such as pur-
chasing clothes or food.

If only everyone could practice and master making rational decisions all the time, wouldn't it be a more orga-
nized world to live in?

FREE BONUSES

P.S. Is it okay if we overdeliver?

Here at Readtrepreneur Publishing, we believe in overdelivering way beyond our reader's expectations. Is it okay if we overdeliver?

Here's the deal, we're going to give you an extremely condensed PDF summary of the book which you've just read and much more…

What's the catch? We need to trust you… You see, we want to overdeliver and in order for us to do that, we've to trust our reader to keep this bonus a secret to themselves? Why? Because we don't want people to be getting our exclusive PDF summaries even without buying our books itself. Unethical, right?

Ok. Are you ready?

Firstly, remember that your book is code: "**READ66**".

Next, visit this link: http://bit.ly/exclusivepdfs

Everything else will be self explanatory after you've visited: http://bit.ly/exclusivepdfs.

We hope you'll enjoy our free bonuses as much as we enjoyed preparing it for you!